# AMY MACDONALD
## THIS IS THE LIFE

www.amymacdonald.co.uk
www.myspace.com/amymacdonald

© 2007 by Faber Music Ltd
First published by Faber Music Ltd in 2007
3 Queen Square, London WC1N 3AU

Arranged by Cat Hopkins
Edited by Lucy Holliday

Logo Design: Fury

Printed in England by Caligraving Ltd
All rights reserved

The text paper used in this publication is a virgin fibre product that is
manufactured in the UK to ISO 14001 standards. The wood fibre used is only
sourced from managed forests using sustainable forestry principles.
This paper is 100% recyclable

ISBN10: 0-571-53096-6
EAN13: 978-0-571-53096-0

Reproducing this music in any form is illegal and forbidden by
the Copyright, Designs and Patents Act, 1988

To buy Faber Music publications or to find out about the full range
of titles available, please contact your local music retailer or
Faber Music sales enquiries:

Faber Music Ltd, Burnt Mill, Elizabeth Way, Harlow, CM20 2HX England
Tel: +44(0)1279 82 89 82 Fax: +44(0)1279 82 89 83
sales@fabermusic.com fabermusic.com

5.   MR ROCK & ROLL
12.  THIS IS THE LIFE
18.  POISON PRINCE
26.  YOUTH OF TODAY
32.  RUN
36.  LET'S START A BAND
43.  BARROWLAND BALLROOM
52.  L.A.
59.  A WISH FOR SOMETHING MORE
68.  FOOTBALLER'S WIFE
76.  THE ROAD TO HOME

81. CALEDONIA (BONUS SONG)

# MR ROCK & ROLL

Words and Music by Amy MacDonald

♩ = 120  **Upbeat**

*Guitar Capo 7th fret*

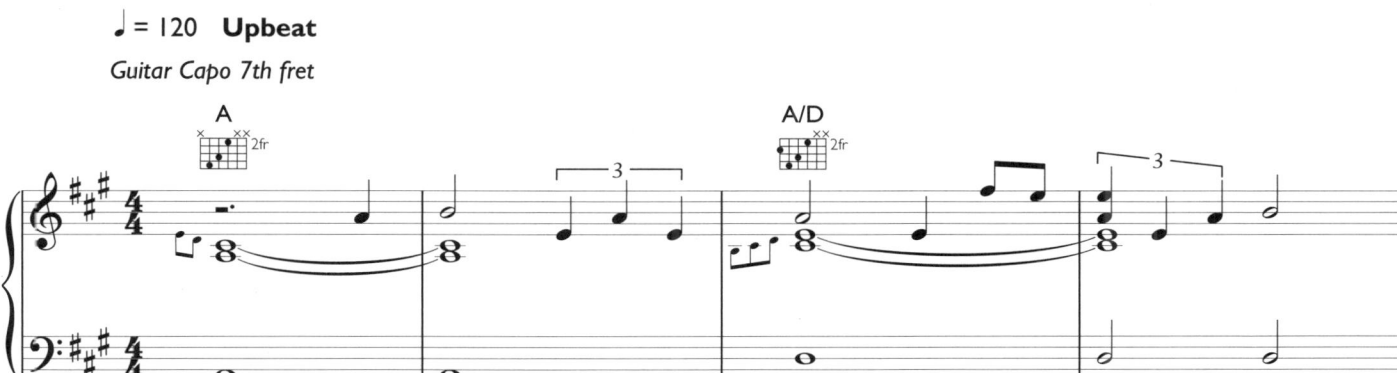
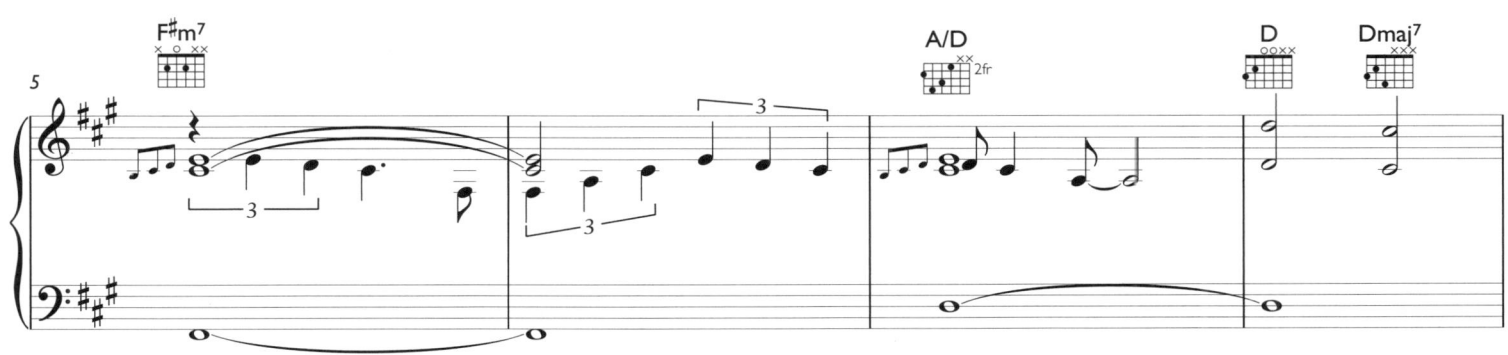
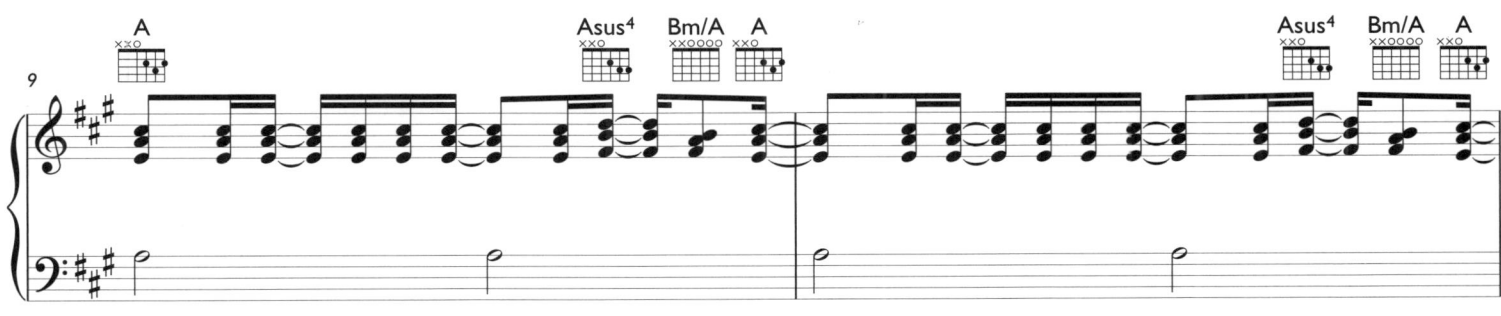
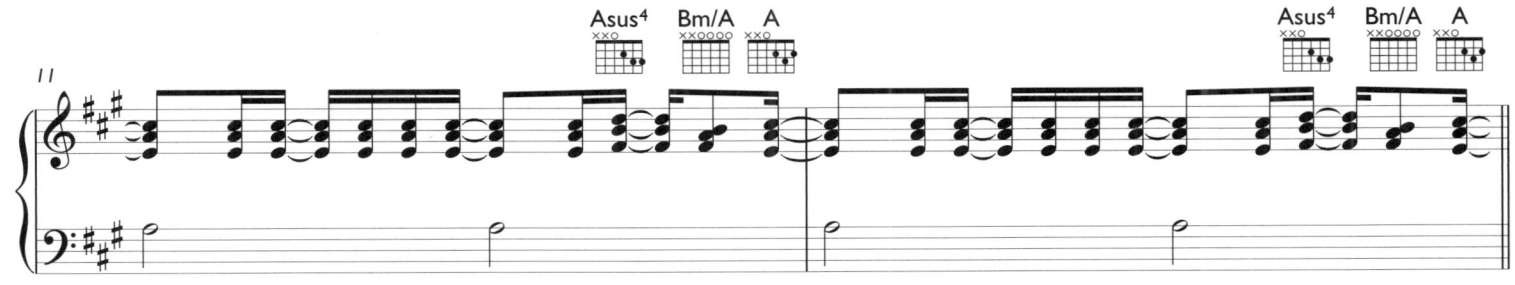

© 2006 Amy MacDonald Ltd
Warner/Chappell Music Publishing Ltd

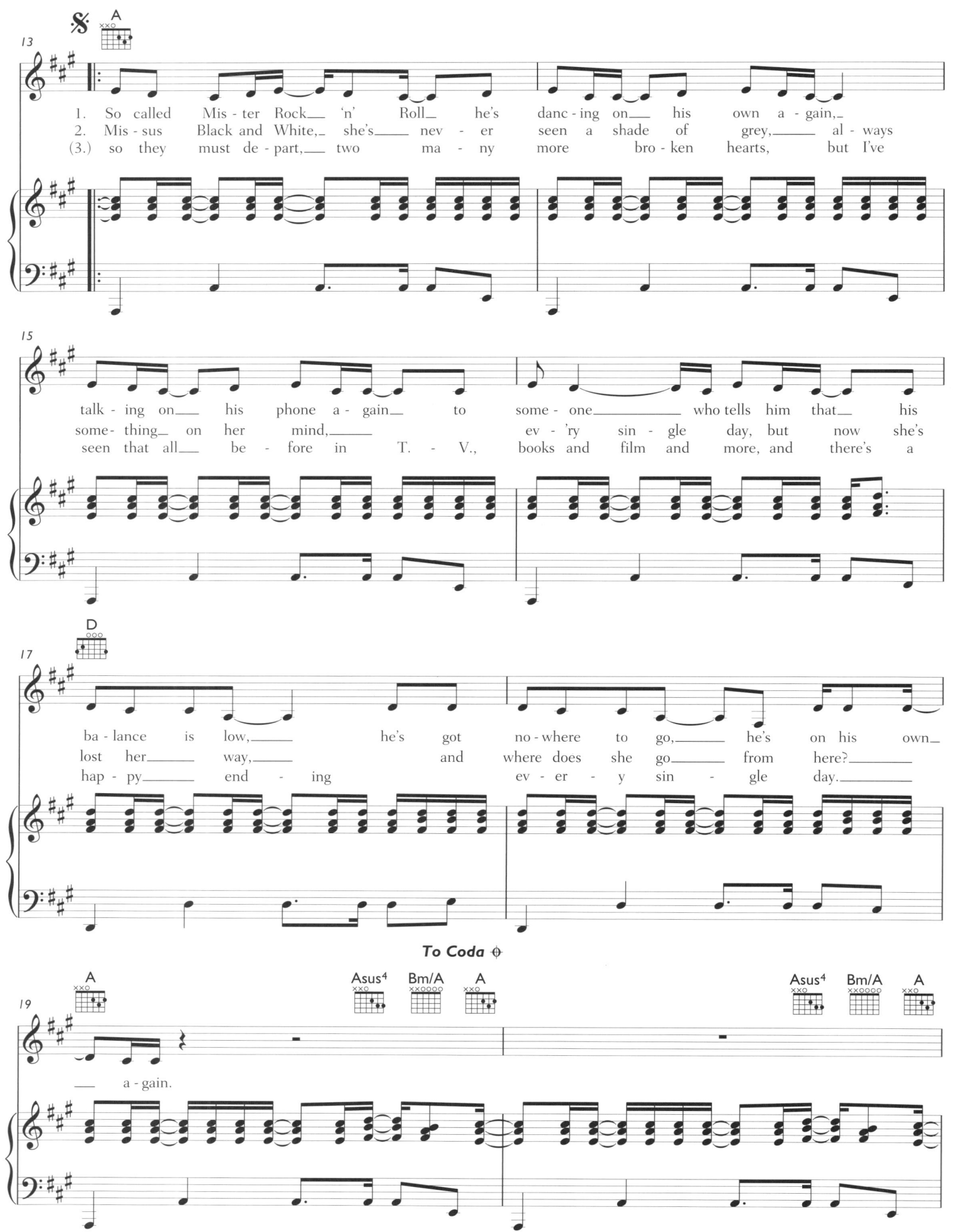

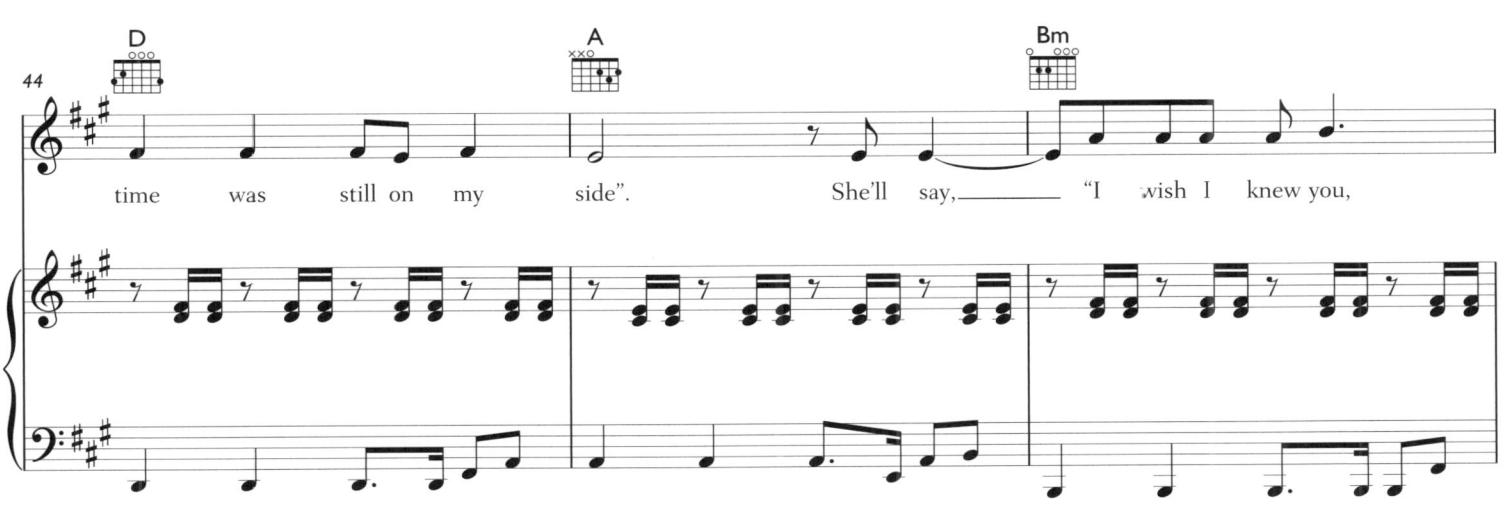

# POISON PRINCE

Words and Music by Amy MacDonald

© 2006 Amy MacDonald Ltd
Warner/Chappell Music Publishing Ltd

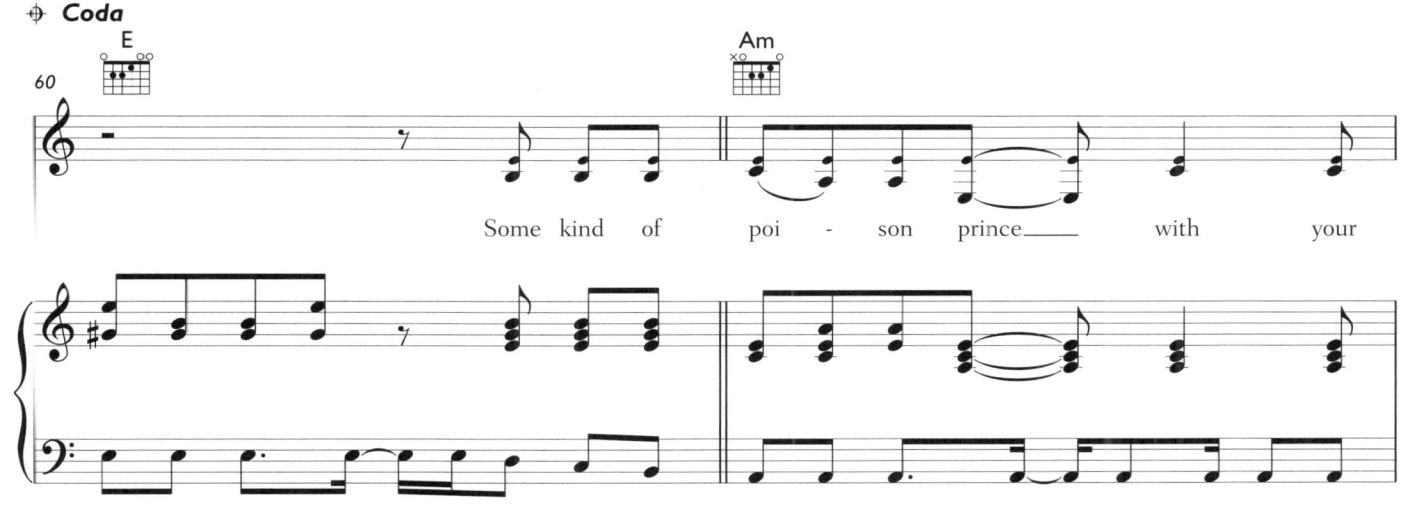

24

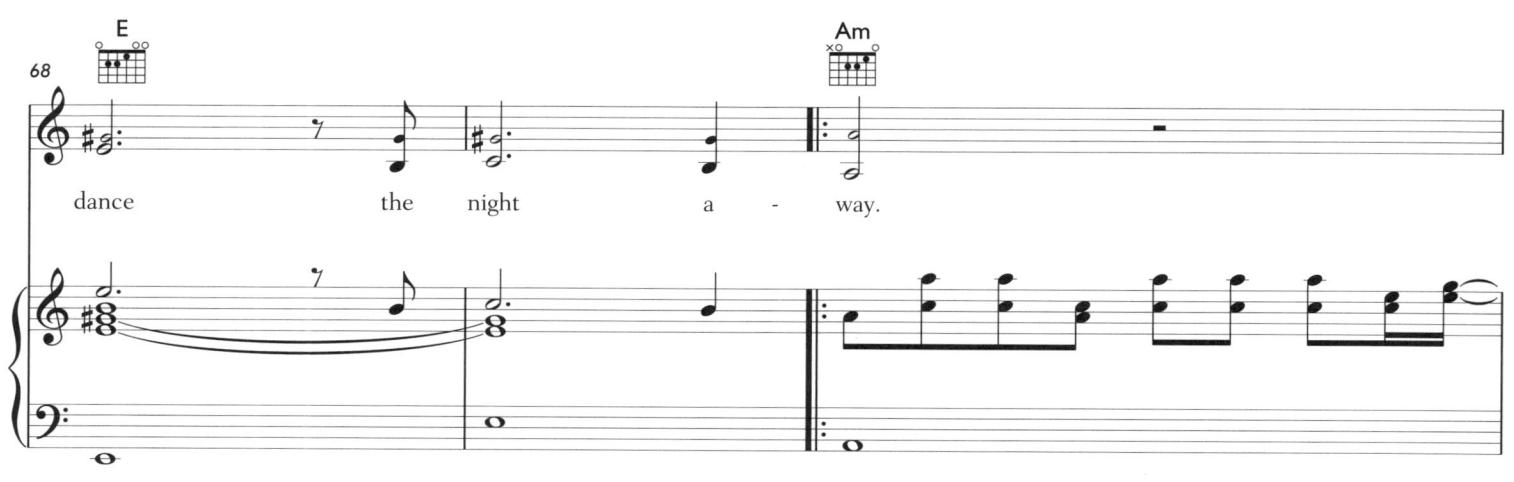

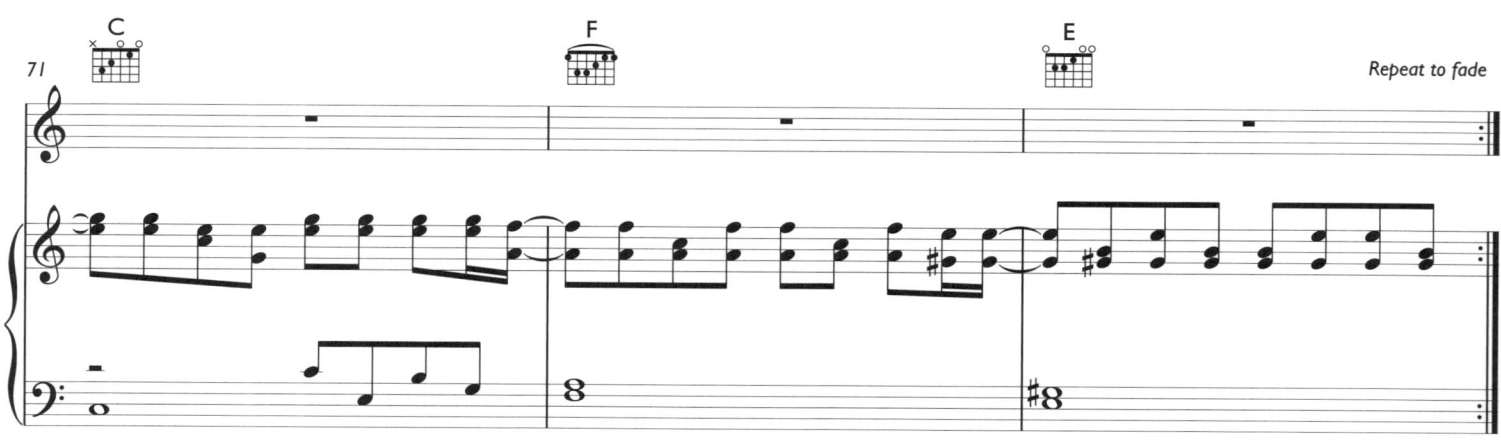

Repeat to fade

# YOUTH OF TODAY

Words and Music by Amy MacDonald

♩ = 90 **Steadily**

*Guitar Capo 5th fret*

1. May-be if you were some spear-head-ed guy I would lis-ten to what you have to say,

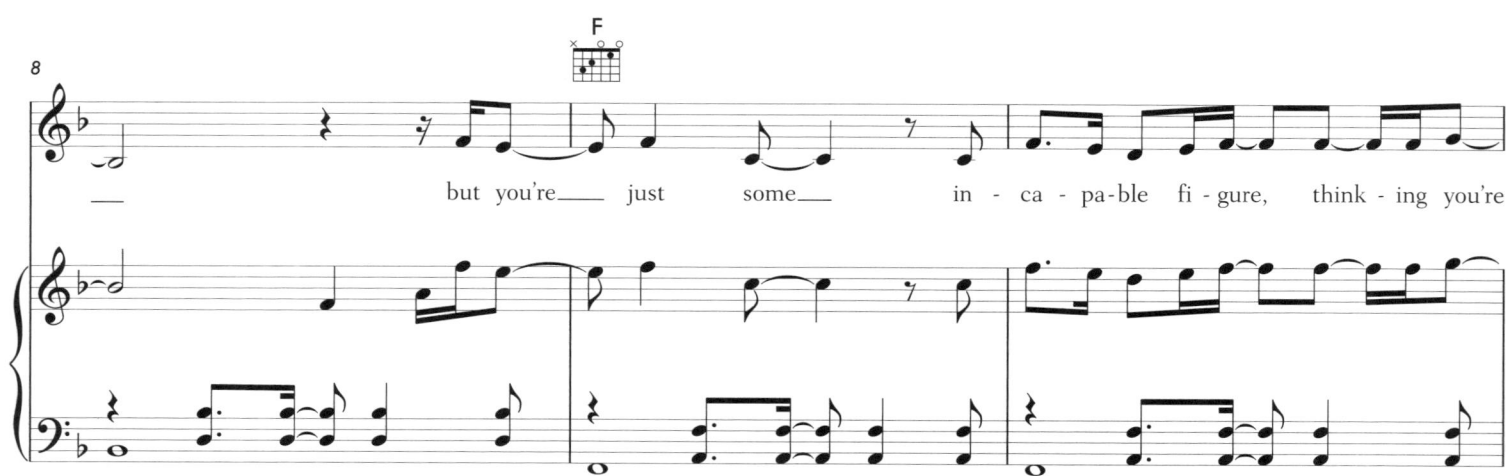

but you're just some in-ca-pa-ble fi-gure, think-ing you're

© 2006 Amy MacDonald Ltd
Warner/Chappell Music Publishing Ltd

# LET'S START A BAND

Words and Music by Amy MacDonald

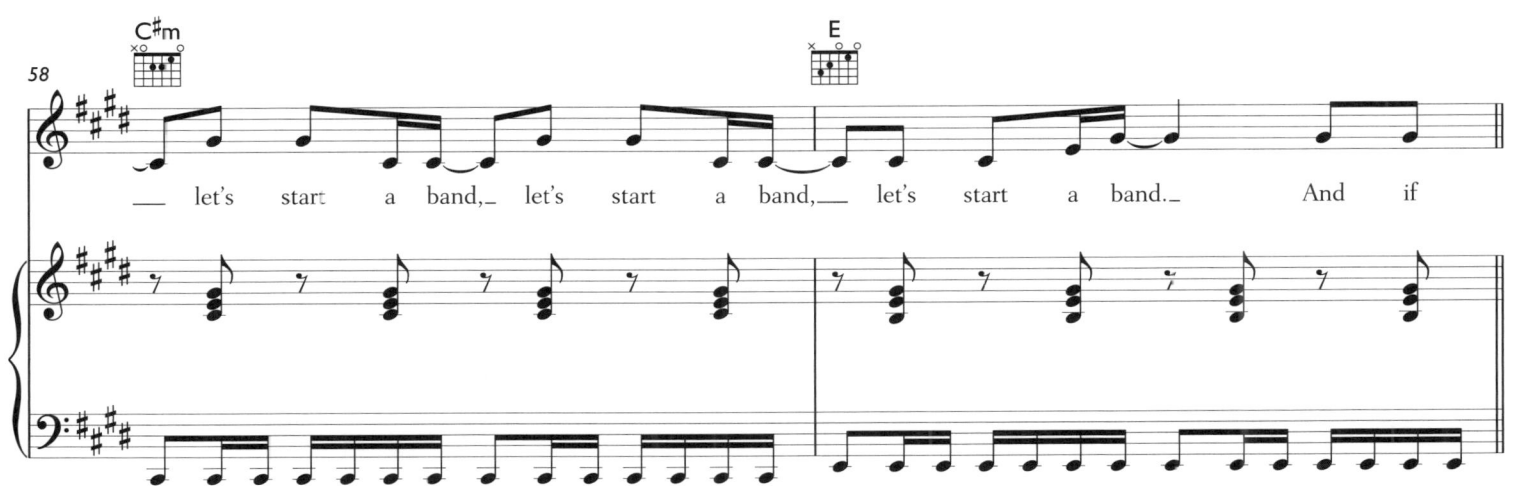

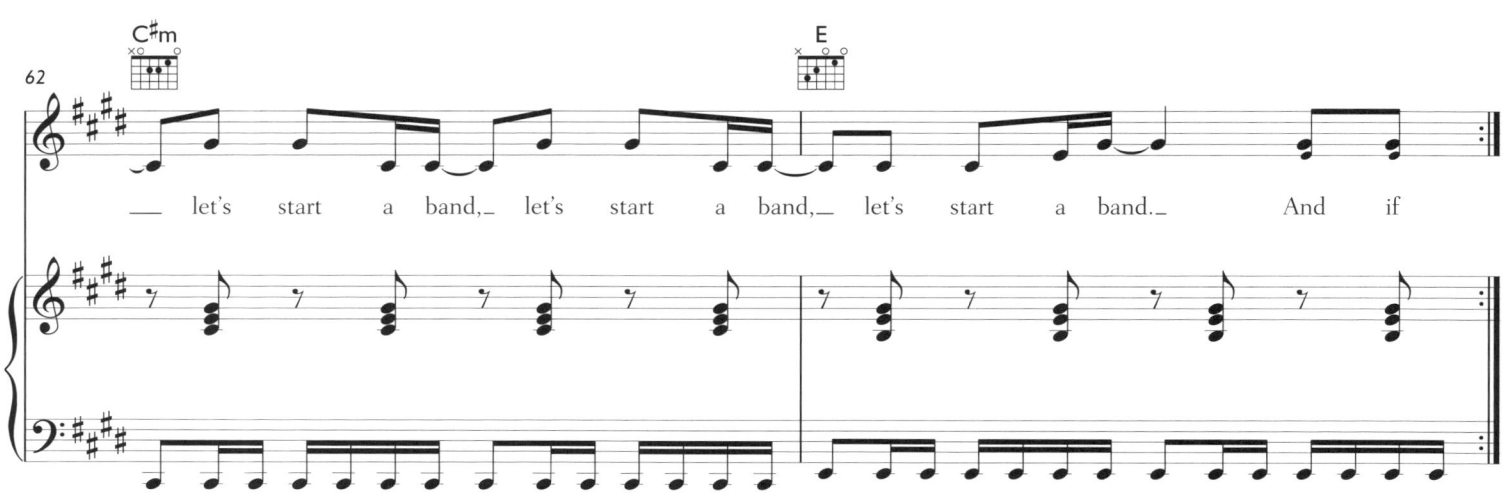
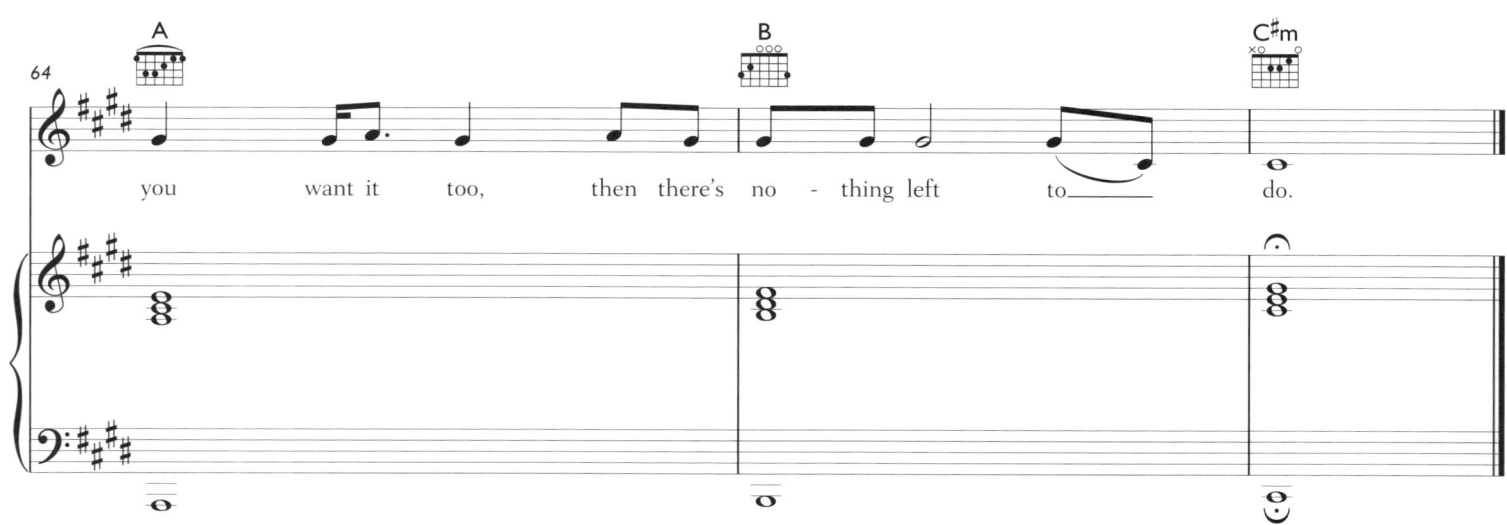

# BARROWLAND BALLROOM

Words and Music by Amy MacDonald

© 2006 Amy MacDonald Ltd
Warner/Chappell Music Publishing Ltd

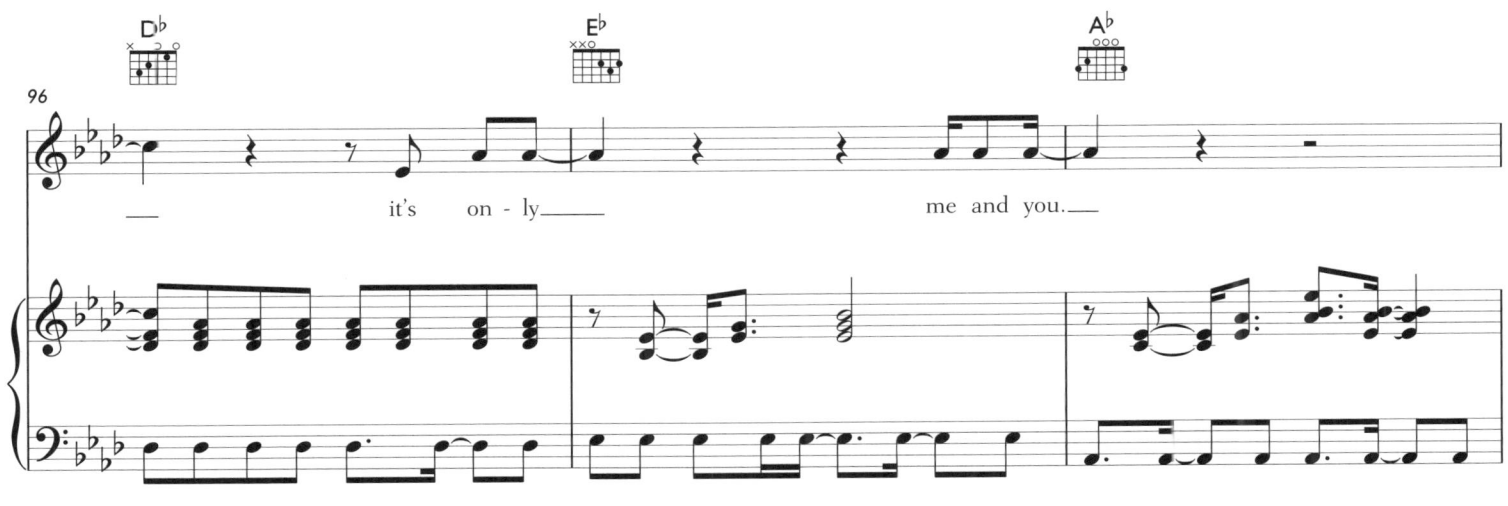

# L.A.

**Words and Music by Amy MacDonald and Peter Wilkinson**

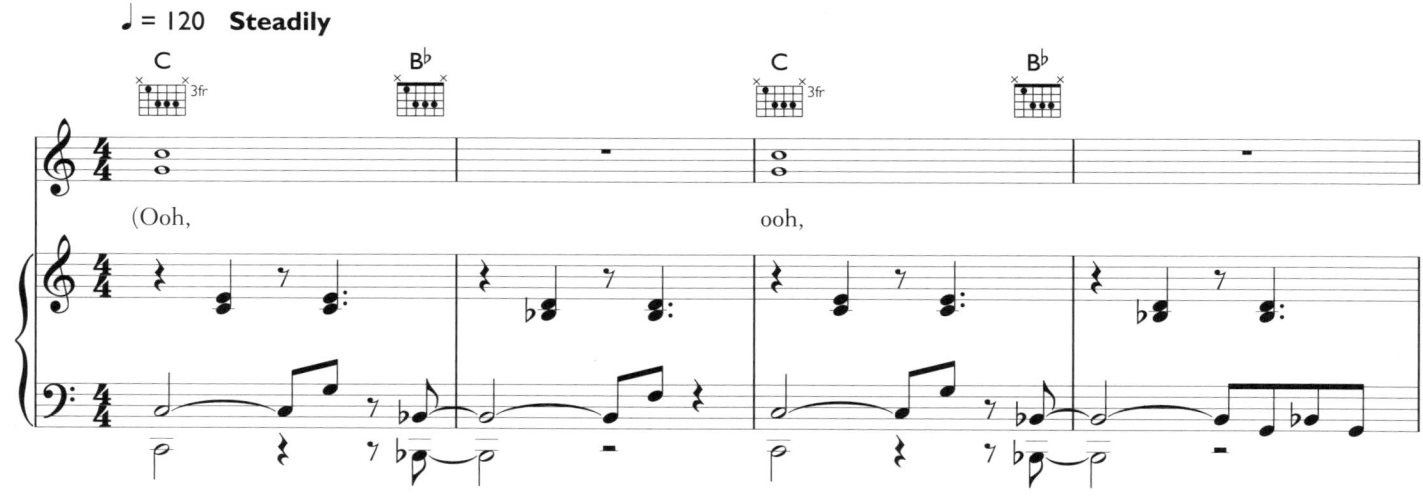

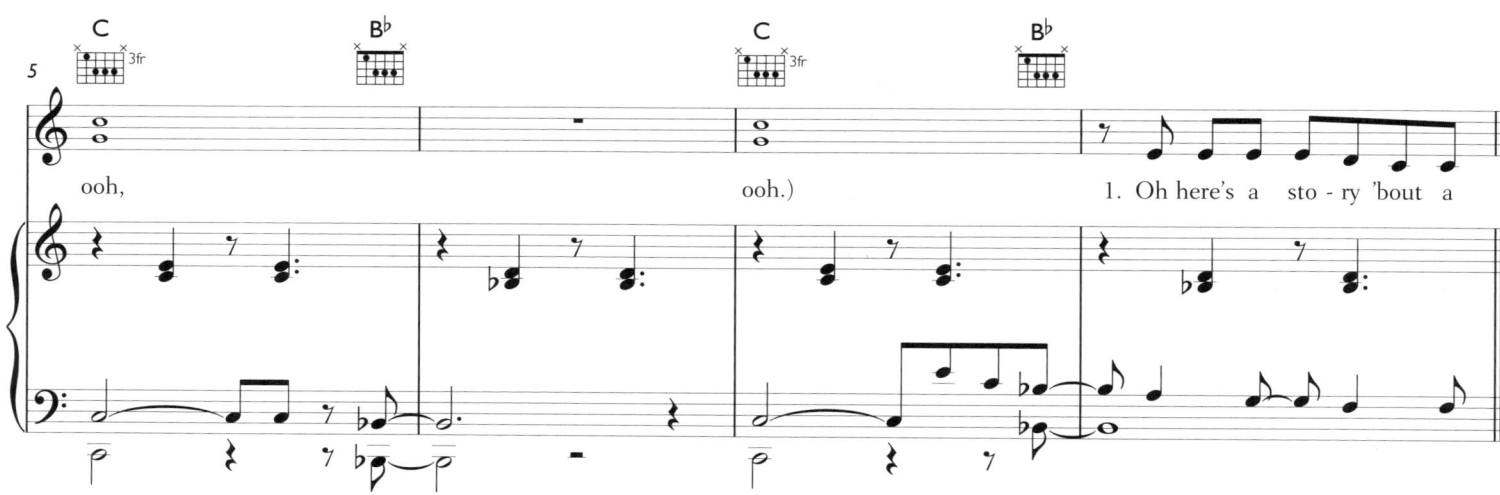

© 2007 Amy MacDonald Ltd and Restless Music Ltd
Warner/Chappell Music Publishing Ltd

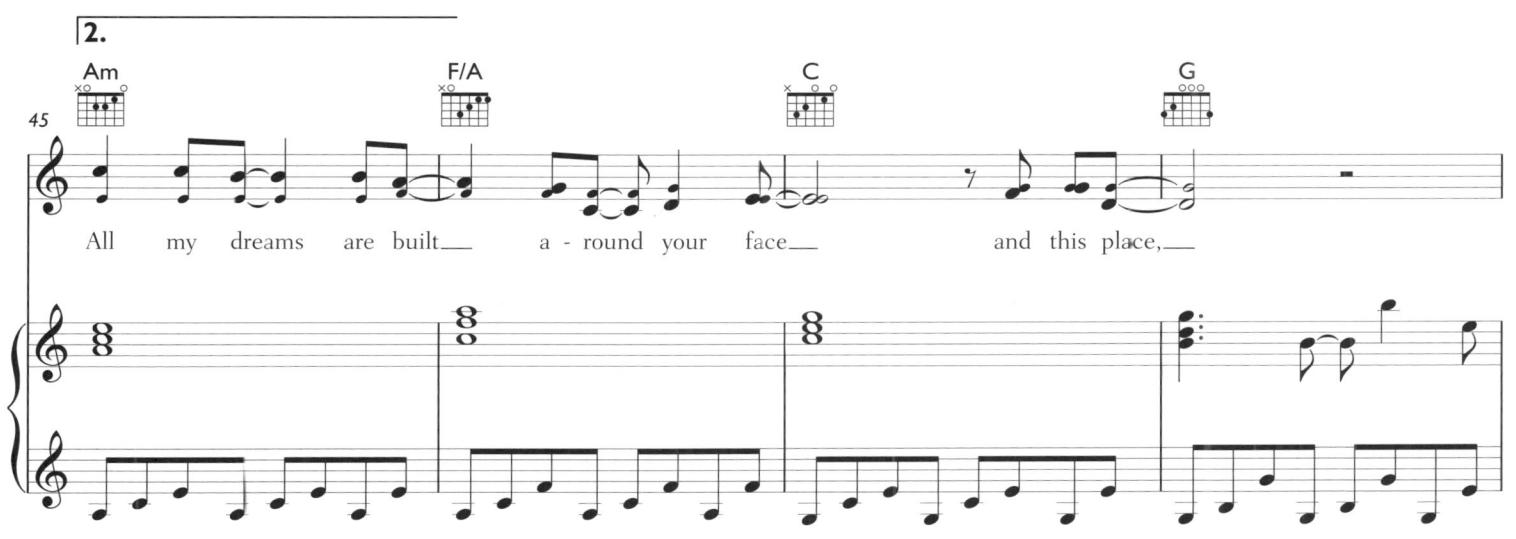

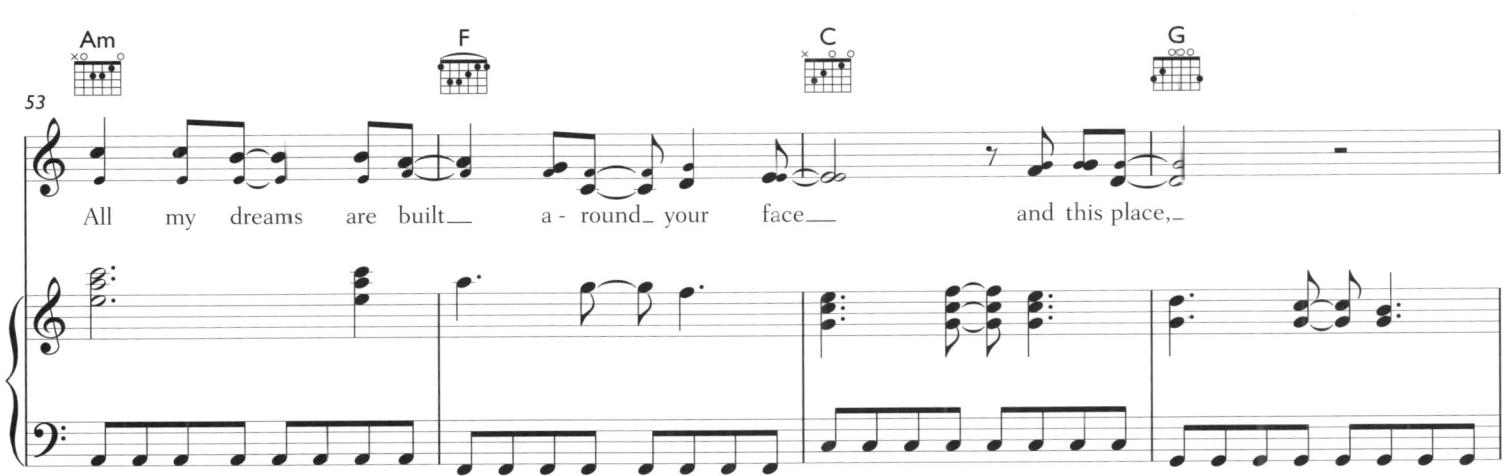

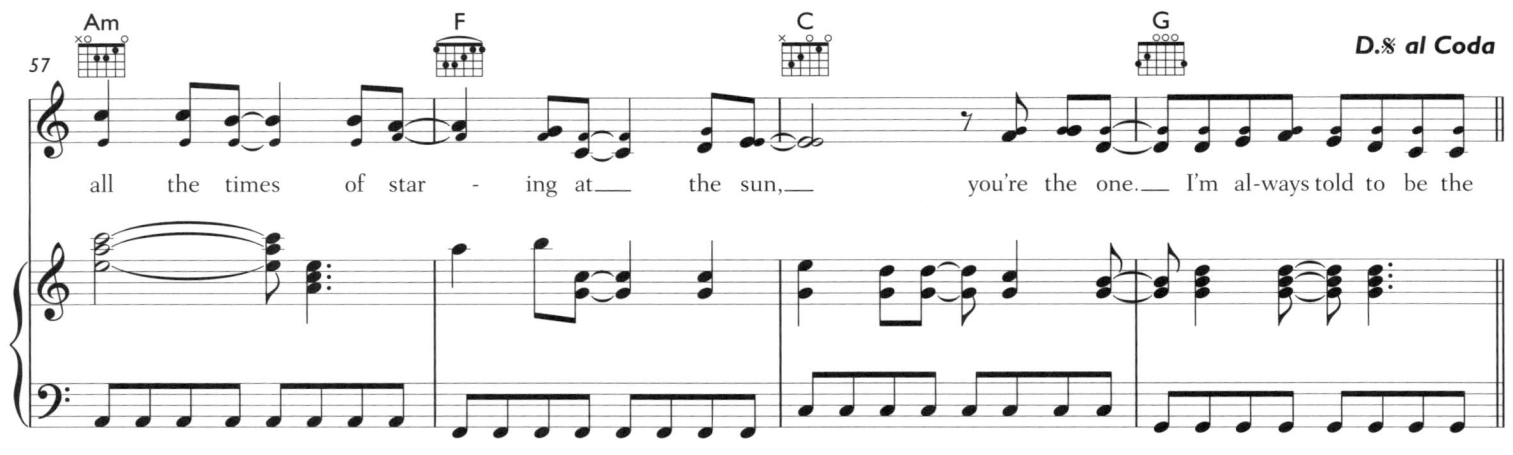
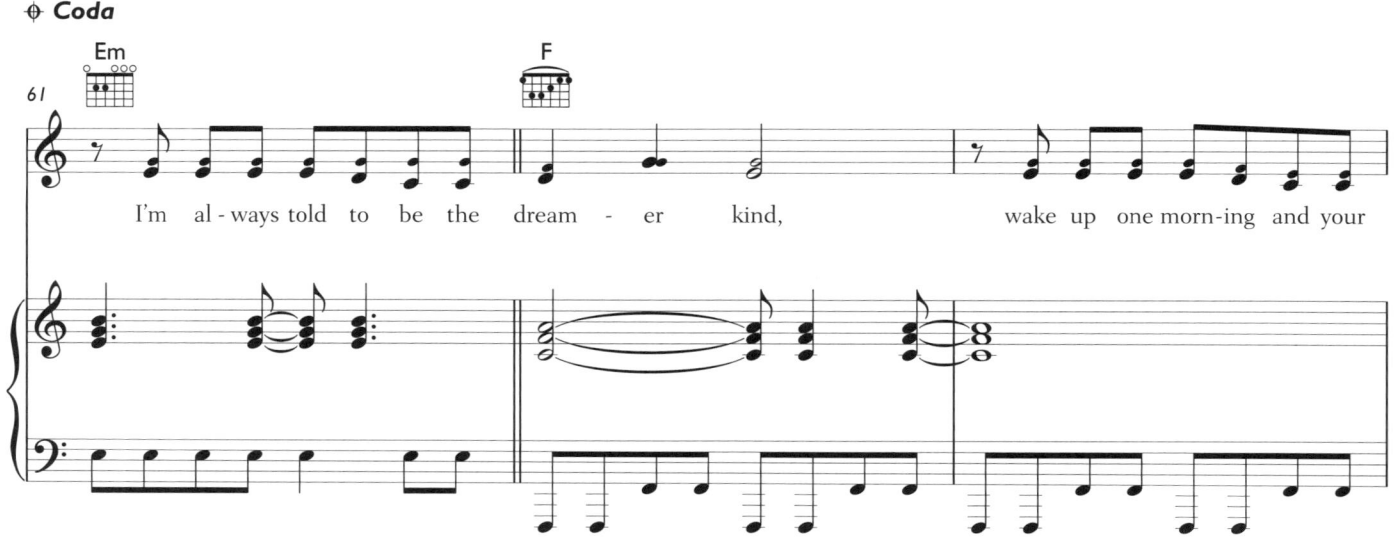
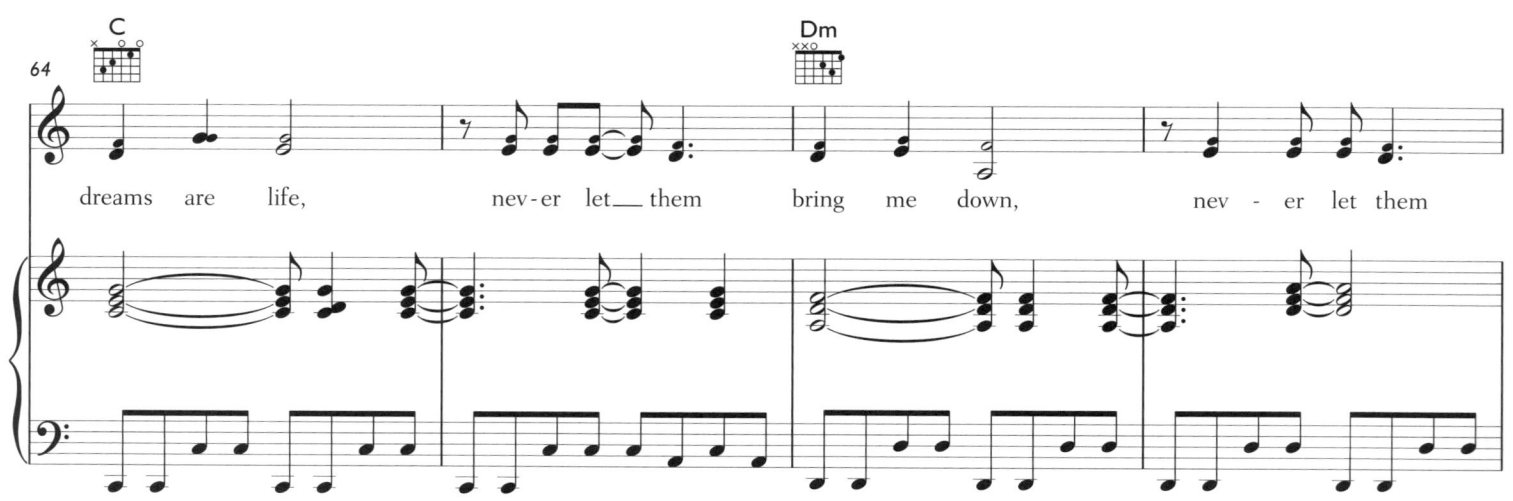

# A WISH FOR SOMETHING MORE

Words and Music by Amy MacDonald

© 2006 Amy MacDonald Ltd
Warner/Chappell Music Publishing Ltd

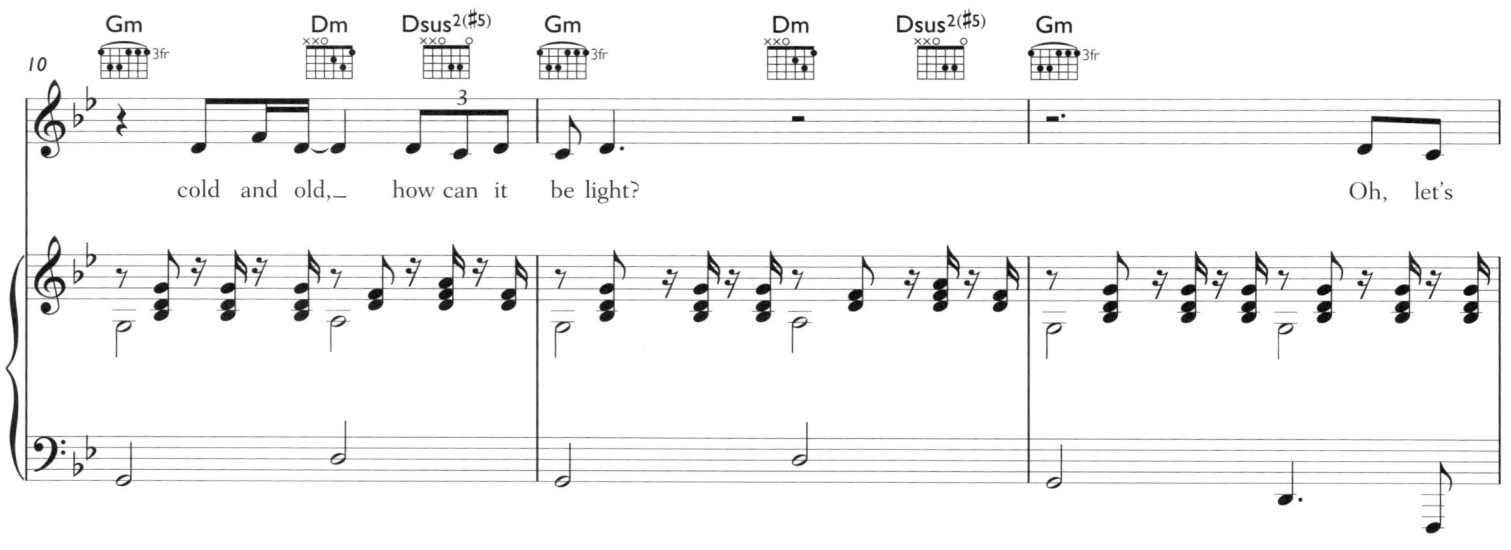

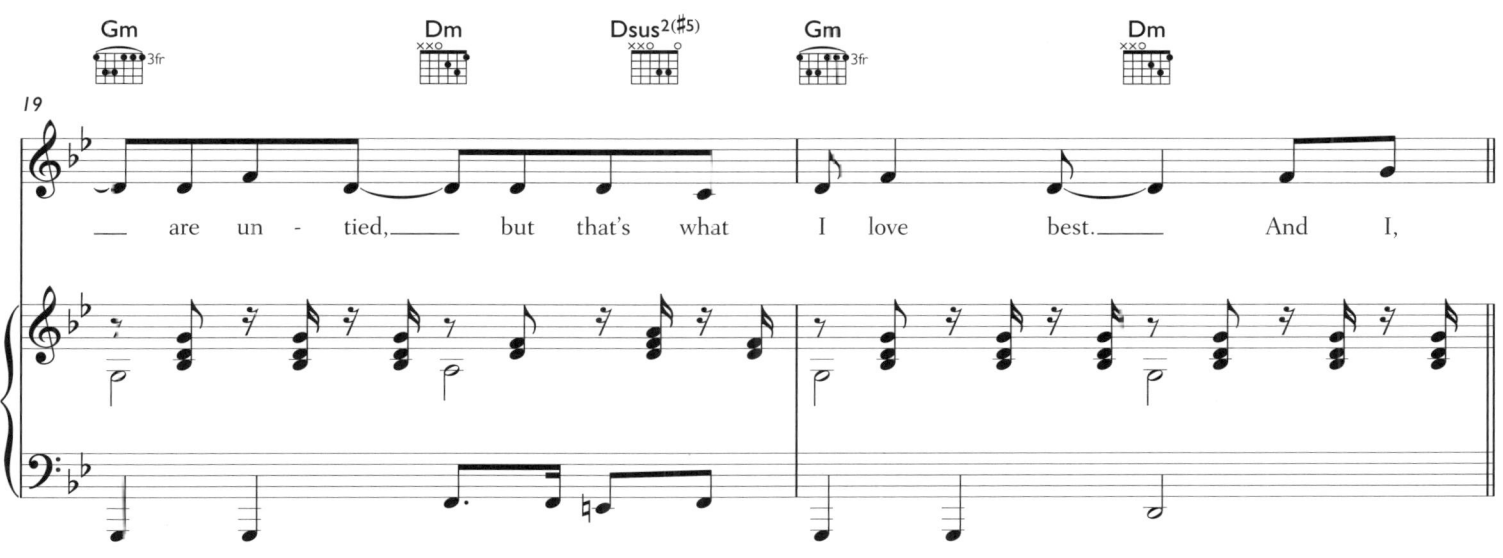

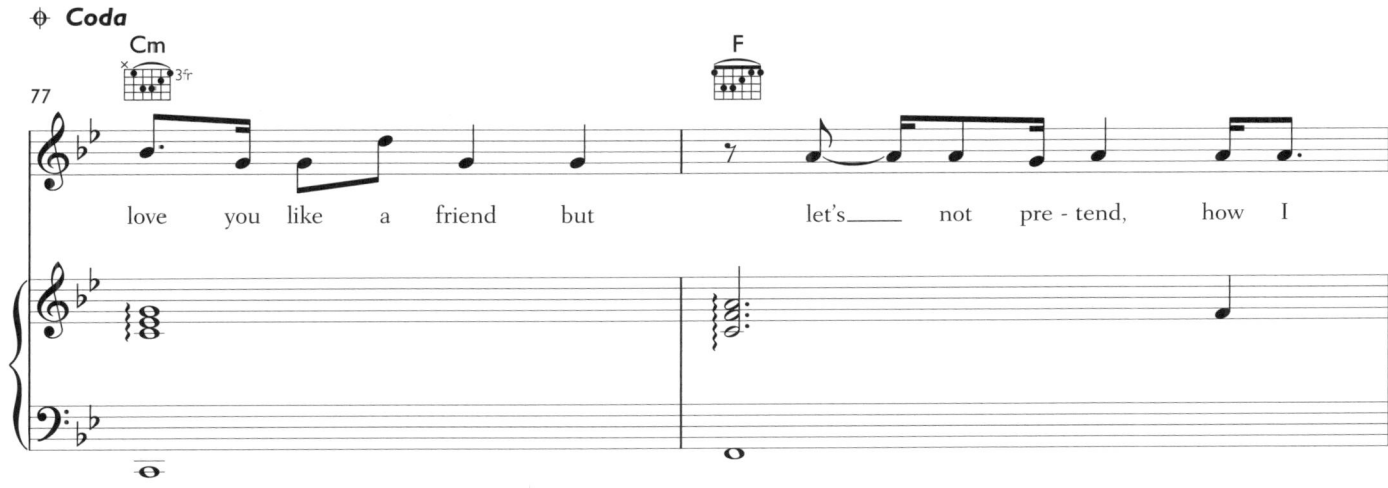

# THE FOOTBALLER'S WIFE

Words and Music by Amy MacDonald

© 2006 Amy MacDonald Ltd
Warner/Chappell Music Publishing Ltd

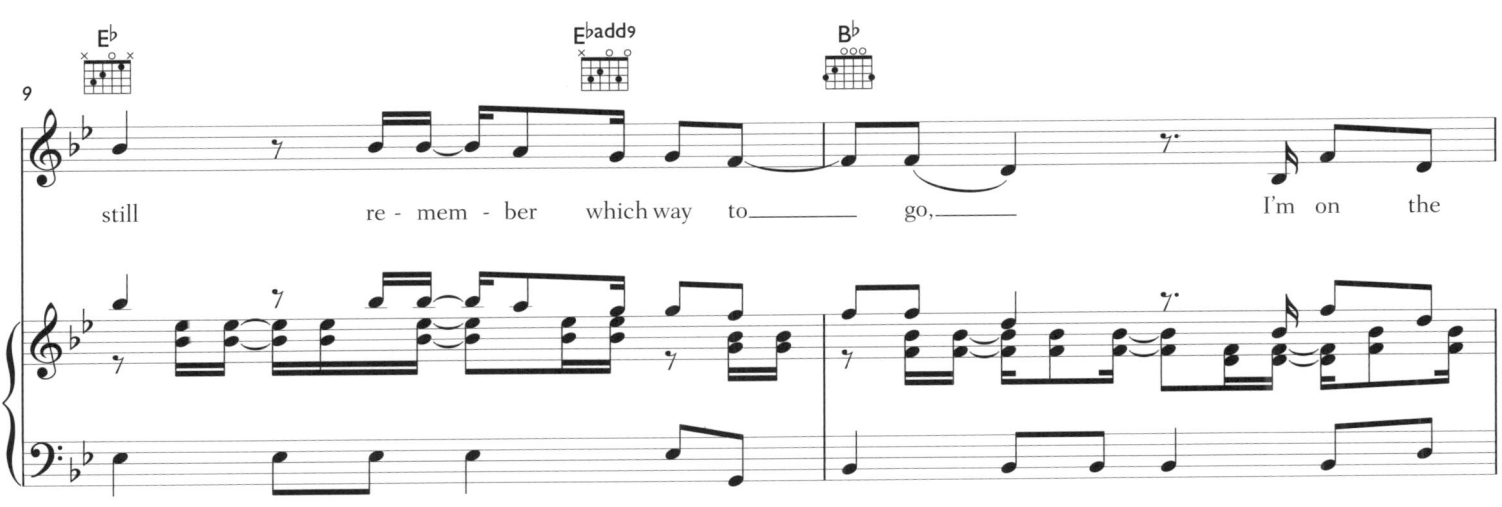

# CALEDONIA
### Words and Music by Dougie MacLean

© 1982 Limetree Arts And Music

THERE'S SO MUCH MORE TO SEE, I DON'T BELIEVE THIS IS HOW THE WORLD SHOULD BE.